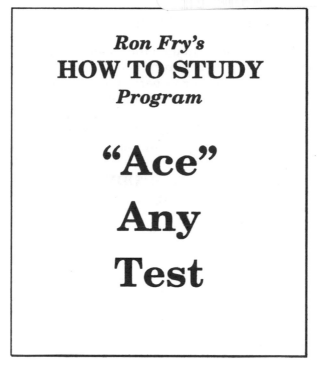

Ron Fry's
HOW TO STUDY
Program

"Ace"
Any
Test

By
Ron Fry

CAREER PRESS
180 Fifth Avenue
P.O. Box 34
Hawthorne, NJ 07507
1-800-CAREER-1
201-427-0229 (outside U.S.)
FAX: 201-427-2037

Ron Fry's HOW TO STUDY *Program*: "Ace" Any Test
ISBN 1-56414-027-X, $5.95
Cover design by Dean Johnson Design, Inc.

To order by this title by mail, please include price as noted above, $2.50 handling per order, and $1.00 for each book ordered. Send to: Career Press, Inc., 180 Fifth Ave., P.O. Box 34, Hawthorne, NJ 07507

Or call Toll-free 1-800-CAREER-1 (Canada: 201-427-0229) to order using VISA or MasterCard, or for further information on books from Career Press.

Library of Congress Cataloging-in-Publication Data
Fry, Ronald W.
    "Ace" any test : / by Ron Fry.
        p. cm. -- (Ron Fry's how to study program)
    Includes index.
    ISBN 1-56414-027-X : $5.95
    1. Examinations--United States--Study guides. 2. Test-taking skills--United States. I. Title. II. Series : Fry, Ronald W. How to study program.
LB3060.57.F79   1992
371.3'02812--dc20   92-13764
                                     CIP

Table of Contents

"Ace"
Any
Test

Introduction
We've Got a Test to Get Ready For   5

Chapter 1
Test Anxiety: The Fear of Fear Itself   7

Chapter 2
Tips for Time Management   14

Chapter 3
Take Notes, Read the Book, Pass the Test   28

Chapter 4
Study Techniques and Test Prep   37

Chapter 5
Essays: Go for Quality, Not Quantity   **49**

Chapter 6
Objective Tests: How to Keep Objective   **57**

Chapter 7
The Day of the Exam: 'Psyching Up'   **70**

Chapter 8
Post-test: Survival and Review   **77**

Chapter 9
How Teachers Make Up Tests   **84**

Index   **92**

Introduction

We've Got a Test to Get Ready For

Jim and Becky react very differently to tests.

Jim gets violently ill *before* the test and Becky has her turn *afterward*. If you know and love someone like Becky or Jim, buy him or her a copy of this book.

Why? Let me give you a quick run-down of what's in it for you (and all the Jims and Beckys who would be here at this moment, but they're running down the hall to the bathroom).

Right away, in Chapter 1, I talk about test anxiety. Maybe you'll be surprised to hear that I don't think you should get rid of all of yours.

Then, in Chapter 2, we look at how you can organize your life so that you don't have to study for the calculus mid-term while brushing your teeth.

The next chapter looks at everything you should be doing all the time so that taking a test doesn't become one of life's worst traumas (matched only by going out to dinner with your parents on a Saturday night and being seen by all your friends).

Chapter 4, my discussion on how to study for a test, deals in mysterious pyramids, wheat and chaff, and my favorite household word, *mnemonics*. Need I say more? (Actually, yes. And I do. In Chapter 4.)

The writer in you is encouraged in Chapter 5, where I give you tips on writing essays. And, since we're talking about writing essays, there's a hint of what's ahead with the "new" SAT (pay special attention if it's in your future).

Chapter 6 takes on the other side of the coin—objective questions. The information here should help you come up with some objective (and correct) answers.

What's the fun of studying for a test if you don't get to take it? All seriousness aside, that's what we'll look at in Chapter 7 when I'll help you get through the "Big Day."

Your life must seem as if it's whizzing by. In Chapter 8, you're suddenly looking at the test you just took in Chapter 7. And I'll share with you some recommendations for keeping up the good work—and improving what wasn't so good.

At last, we come to Chapter 9, the test from the teacher's point of view. It's a little like military strategy: Know as much about the enemy as possible.

And I wrap it up with an easy fill-in-the-blank form you can use to help you with the whole process, including an evaluation of how you did.

So, why are you waiting? We've got a test to get ready for!

Chapter 1

Test Anxiety: The Fear of Fear Itself

"Life is a test. If you woke up alive this morning, it means you got an 'A' for yesterday." —Ron Fry

"All we have to fear is fear itself."
—Franklin Delano Roosevelt

"A little anxiety never hurt anyone." —your mother

FDR was *almost* right. The only thing you *may* have to fear is fear itself. But, frankly, you *don't* have to. You just have to conquer it or beat it into submission so that you can get on with your life—and with your biology exam.

Your mother is right, too. OK, so she isn't the person you want to pick out your clothes or coordinate your social life. But she's right about one thing: It doesn't hurt to have a little anxiety. You don't want to become so complacent that you lose that "edge" that you need.

Let's spend a few minutes talking about why tests scare people, and then let's help you spend your time studying instead of wasting it on anxiety attacks.

Even famous people do it

I still remember a documentary on a famous singer that I saw on TV years ago. The camera had been following her around while she went to rehearsal, got her make-up on, and talked with her manager.

The scene I remember most was the shot of her as she waited backstage to be announced. Now, remember, this was a woman who had been wowing them for decades. You could hear the audience: It was excited to be in her presence. It was friendly. And she—standing in the wings as the announcer called out her name to loud applause—looked nervous, horrified, petrified, regretful that she'd ever entered show business and extremely vulnerable. And this from a person who knew she was being filmed.

But, when the announcer called her name and the roar of applause began, she was transformed. She walked with a determined gait to the stage, the lights hit her, she smiled and took the microphone, the band began and she never looked back. Her famous voice filled the auditorium, and the audience went wild. If she had those little panics and still passed the test, why shouldn't you?

A little tension goes a long way

Truly successful entertainers or public speakers will usually admit they get those little knots in their stomachs just before they have to perform. And they would be the first ones to tell you that not only is it OK to go through a nervous moment or two, they actually prefer that—it gives them the adrenaline rush they need to do a good job.

Let's put that back into the context of your exam-taking: You may have taken a test in the past where you thought you knew everything, did little if any studying—and got a bad grade. Don't go too far the other way.

But don't get too tensed up either. Keep a little anxiety in your life. Just keep it under control and in perspective.

Why is there terror present in the first place? Because we don't want to fail. We realize that, within the next 30 or 60 minutes, a percentage of our grade will be determined by what we write or *don't* write down on a piece of paper, or which box we color in with our No. 2 pencil.

Why fail?

Now, why do some people fail? Maybe they don't study. Or don't pay attention. Or they studied the wrong thing.

Sometimes, it's the old Fear of Success. "Gee," you think to yourself, "if I do well on this exam, my parents will expect me to do well on the next exam—and the teacher will think I'm going to start doing well every day!"

Fear of success, like martyrdom, is boring. Look at it this way: You'll always have pressure on you throughout your life, so you might as well have *good* pressure ("Hey, genius, keep up the good work!") rather than *bad* pressure ("I can't understand how anyone with a brain like yours makes such bad grades!")

Forget about Sally

One more reason for failure? Some people can't deal with competition. All they can think about is what Sally is

9

doing. Look at her! She's sitting there, writing down one answer after another—and you just know they're all correct!

Who cares about Sally? Only one person in that room should be concerned with Sally and Sally's performance. That's right. Just as only one person should be concerned with *your* performance. Make it all a game: Compete with yourself. See if you can't beat your previous test scores. Now, that's positive competition!

You don't have to join the club

Some people thrive on their own misery and are jealous if you don't thrive on it too. They want to include you in all of their hand-wringing situations, whether you really know (or care) what's happening. These are people to avoid when you're preparing for an exam—the Anxiety Professionals.

"Oh, I'll never learn all this stuff!" they'll cry. You might not win points with Miss Manners if you say, "Well, if you'd shut up and study, you might!" You *can* have the pleasure of thinking it—on your way to a quiet place to study alone.

And watch out for those "friends" who call you the night before the exam with, "I just found out we have to know Chapter 12!" Don't fall into their trap. Instead of dialing 911, calmly remind them that the printed sheet the professor passed out two weeks ago clearly says, "Test on Chapters 6 through 11." Then hang up, get on with your life, and let them wring their hands all the way to the bottom of the grading sheet.

Focus on the exam

If you have trouble concentrating on your preparations for the exam, try this: Think of your life as a series of shoe boxes (the Imelda Marcos Theory). The boxes are all open and lined up in a nice, long, neat row. In each shoe box is a small part of your life—school, work, romantic interest, hobbies, *ad florsheim.* Although you have to move little pieces from one box to another from time to time, you can—and should—keep a lot of this stuff as separate as possible.

While your parents try—but don't always succeed—in obeying the admonition, "Don't bring work home from the office," you can be certain to obey this one: "Don't take your life's worries into the chemistry final."

Is there life after this test?

Yes. And, furthermore, isn't there life *before* this test? Tests are important. They tell the teacher and you how well you're doing in the class (and how well he or she is doing). How many correct answers you get will help you understand how well you know the material.

But, all that aside, a test is only a part of your life. Any one test is not going to ruin your life, it's only going to give you the opportunity to produce a certain grade.

Do your best, using the tips I'm sharing with you in this book, and go forward. And don't, in the process of preparing for an exam, decide that all other forms of life must cease. Maybe you can't devote as much of your time to soaps (but you can tape them for a post-test reward) or even perhaps to those closest to you, but relationships (and soap operas) go on, long after the exams are forgotten.

You're already an expert

You've already taken lots and lots of tests: pop quizzes, oral exams, standardized tests, tests on chapters and units and whole books—and whole semesters. You've done this for years. And, for the most part, you've been successful. And, if you haven't always been as successful as you'd like, keep on reading. For the remainder of this book, we're going to review what you can do to change all that. All this experience, coupled with the real-life "tests" I've already mentioned, demonstrate that you're pretty good—even excellent. Stop a moment and pat yourself on the back. You're a successful test-taker, in spite of a little fright here and there.

One in a million

Just admitting that you're not at ground zero can help you realize that preparing for an exam is not in itself a whole new Task of Life—it's merely part of a continuum.

Think of this fraction: 1 over 1 million. Your life is the big number. This next test is the little number. All the "ones" in your life add up to the 1 million, thus they are important, but, all by themselves, they can't compare to the Giant Economy Number of Life. Write "1/1,000,000" at the top of your next test to remind yourself of that. That alone should kill off a bunch of stomach butterflies.

"Extra" tests give extra help

Here's another tried-and-true suggestion: If you want to practice the many recommendations you're going to get in this book, including what I'm sharing with you in this important first chapter, take a few "extra" tests just to give yourself some practice. It will also help you with overcoming the unacceptable levels of test anxiety.

Get permission from your teachers to retake some old tests to practice the test-taking techniques and exorcising, once and for all, the High Anxiety Demon. And take a couple standardized tests that your counseling office might have, too, since the color-in-the-box answer sheets and serious questions in printed form have their own set of rules (which, as you can guess, we'll talk about later in this book).

Anxiety quotient

To come to terms with the "importance" of a test, read the list below. Knowing the answers to as many of these questions as possible will help reduce your anxiety.

1. What material will the exam cover?
2. How many total points are possible?
3. What percentage of my semester grade is based on this exam?
4. How much time will we have to take the exam?
5. Where will the exam be held?
6. What kinds of questions will be on the exam (matching, multiple-choice, essay, true/false....)?
7. How many points will be assigned to each question? Will essay questions count for 25 percent of the exam or 50 percent? Will there be five multiple-choice questions or 105?
8. Will it be an open-book exam?
9. What can I take in with me? Calculator? Candy bar? Other material crucial to my success?
10. Will I be penalized for wrong answers?

Take a hike

Finally, to shake off pre-test anxiety, take a walk. Or a vigorous swim. In the days before an exam, no matter how "big" it is, don't study too hard or all the time or you'll walk into the exam with a fried brain.

Chapter 2

Tips for Time Management

"Work expands so as to fill the time available for its completion." —Cyril Parkinson, Parkinson's Law

"If you have time to watch that stupid TV show, you have time to clean your room." —your mother

Poor time. It really gets a bum rap. In this chapter, let's look at how we can organize our lives so that we have enough time for everything: School, family and friends, work and studying (and, oh yes, even cleaning your room).

Let's start by making a major adjustment in our thinking: Time is our friend, not our enemy. Time allows us space in each day or week or month to do a lot of fun things and to reach certain milestones in order to advance our career, get diplomas or degrees, establish and develop relationships, go on vacations and all that. And it allows us to prepare for tests. (Let's not get carried away and forget the focus of this book.) This chapter includes some simple time charts that will help you work on *when* and *where* and *how* you manage the various demands on your time.

And, for a whole book on the subject, don't forget that I've already written **Manage Your Time**, one of the six other books in my **HOW TO STUDY Program**. (Look at the back of this book for a complete list of them.) While this chapter concentrates on studying for tests, **Manage Your Time** outlines ways that will help you in even more detail, and covers even more aspects of your life as a student.

The management of time

"Time management" has become a big business in America. You can find a course on this topic in the catalog of any community college or adult-education program in the country. Some corporations send their entire work force to take time management seminars.

Stick with me. Instead of paying hundreds of dollars for such a course, pay close attention to what's in this chapter (and, as I just said, for even more detail, read **Manage Your Time**).

Look at it this way: Between now and next Tuesday, whether you are preparing to play in the state basketball tournament, writing a paper on the Mississippi Delta or holding down three jobs (or, heaven help you, all of the above), you have exactly the same amount of time as the rest of us. It's what you *do* with that time that makes the difference.

How are you going to get from here to then? Are you just going to go crashing along, like an elephant trampling down banana trees? Or are you going to get there with a plan? Good. That's the right answer. (See? You just passed *another* test. Congratulations.)

The vital statistics

How often have you made a "to-do" list and then either forgotten it, lost it or ignored it? To-do lists have incredible merits if you do them right. But they're not much good if you don't use them.

Let's run through the composition and execution of a to-do list for a shopping expedition as an example. Here's what I do when I am making up a list of run-around-town errands:

First, after writing down where I have to go, I turn the paper over and make individual lists of items for each stopping place. I may have Smith's Drugstore on the "where to go" front side of the list, but on the back I have listed shaving cream, bubble gum, newspaper, hair spray, prescription.

Am I (A) compulsive-obsessive or (B) merely organized?

If this were a real test, the right answer would be (B).

By separating the *where* from the *what*, I am able to focus on getting from the post office to the drugstore to the hardware store without trying to separate the toothpaste from the tool kit. On the other hand, when I am heading down Aisle 3B, I can concentrate on what items I need from this particular stop.

I number the *where* side (putting a "1" beside my first stop, a "2" by the second and on and on) so that I can do a "no brainer"—I have quickly figured out in what order I need or want to do the shopping, and I don't have to stop to think where to go next. I just consult the list.

I devised this simple addition to my list-making because I had spent too many Saturday mornings driving back and forth in an almost random fashion or sitting in a parking lot saying to myself, "Now, where should I go next? The drugstore? No, that's near the video store. That means I should..."

Take a whole five seconds at home and write down the 1, 2, 3, etc., and then go for it.

I do one more thing on my shopping list: If I need to take anything with me (return a video, drop off cleaning, take an article to be photocopied, etc.), I place a "T" with a circle around it beside the place I need the "T" item for. That way, I don't get to Smith's only to discover that I forgot to bring the prescription form. (If convenient, put all the "T" items, along with the list, beside the door so you won't have to go searching for them when it's time to leave.)

Now, why am I sharing all this detailed information on my shopping-list habits when we're supposed to be talking about getting ready for your zoology exam? Because the methods and the rationale are similar to your management of time. Here's what my list does for me:

- I don't forget anything.
- I save time.
- It's quick and easy.
- I "save" my brain for what's important.

Attention, Study-Mart shoppers!

Think of the time between now and your next exam as your shopping trip. You want to use this time most effectively so that (1) you don't forget anything, (2) you work efficiently (save time), (3) you arrange your studying so that it's done as quickly and as easily as possible, and (4) you concentrate on the important details, not on *all* details (big difference!).

How much time do you have? Unless I missed something in the paper this morning, we all have 24 hours a day. But you and I know that's not what we're talking about here. We have to subtract sleeping, eating, commuting and obligations like work and classes...whoa! Any time left?

Sure there is. But, first, you need to get a handle on what you *must* do, what you *should* do and what you *want* to do. Let's refer to them as our H, M and L priorities.

The H ("High") priorities are those things we *must* do between now and the next test.

The M ("Medium") priorities are those things we *should* do, but we could postpone without being jailed or written out of the will.

The L ("Low") priorities are those things we live for but are *expendable*. At least, they're expendable until you've finished taking this next exam.

Yes, Virginia, it's all right to sleep

Examples?

An "H" is sleeping and eating and attending class, especially the class in question. (You simply can't ignore these.)

An "M" is getting your family car's oil changed or taking your cat to the vet for a check-up. (Important, but unless the car's dipstick shows that it has no oil or the cat is so sick it's trying to dial the vet itself, these tasks can be delayed for a handful of days.)

An "L" is going to the Hitchcock Film Festival or partying with friends up at the cabin in the mountains.

In *Manage Your Time*, I gave you three different forms to use. I'm including them in this book as well. The first one, the Term Planning Calendar, helps you sort out and manage the big picture. The second, Priority Tasks This Week, breaks the semester down to seven-day periods. And the third, Daily Schedule, will reduce it to a focused day-by-day format.

These charts are intended to cover all aspects of your life from social events to final exams. Another chart I provided for you in that book is called a Projects Board and it deals with all the necessary steps to start, work on and complete a project (a term paper, committee work and review/exam schedules).

Let's look again at these forms in light of preparing for and taking tests:

An endearing term

Let's talk about the Term Planning Calendar, on page 20, first. Simply put, this is a series of monthly calendars with all the important events listed on them. Sounds pretty simple. Actually, it is. Even if you've only got six weeks left in the semester, go ahead and fill out one of these.

Don't just list the school-related items ("Biology Semester Exam, 9 a.m." on May 3); put down the "H" items from the rest of your life, too ("Trip to Chicago" on March 22).

One very good reason for listing all the social/personal/non-academic items is for you to determine which of those are going to remain in the "H" category. For example, if you discover that you have planned a trip to Chicago for the weekend before your French mid-term the following Monday, you'd better cry *"Sacre bleu!"* and decide the Chicago trip is an "L" and must be moved to another time.

Get the picture?

One of the most important reasons for writing down what exactly is coming up is to get that Big Picture. Once you've filled in all the due dates of term papers, unit tests,

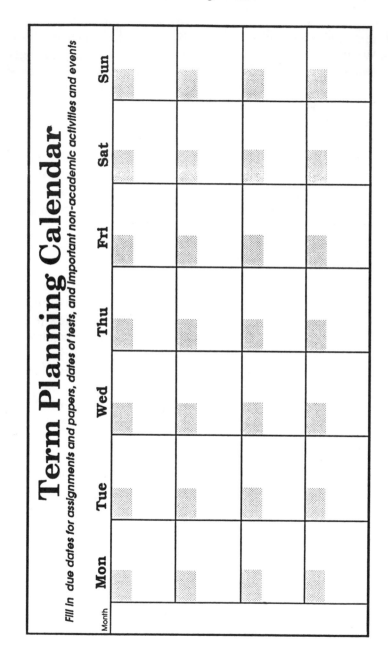

Term Planning Calendar

Fill in due dates for assignments and papers, dates of tests, and important non-academic activities and events

Month	Mon	Tue	Wed	Thu	Fri	Sat	Sun

mid-terms, finals, project reports, etc., take a good look at the results.

Are there a bunch of deadlines in the same week or even on the same day? During finals and mid-terms, of course, this really can't be helped and there's no way to take the tests at another time.

But perhaps you can do something about some of the other deadlines. If you have a French test covering three units on the same day that you have to turn in a paper on the "Influence of the Beatles on British Foreign Policy" and a status report on your gerbil project for sociology, take the plunge and decide that you will get the paper and the project status report done early so that you can devote the time just prior to that day to studying for your French test.

You can't make decisions like that, however, if you can't sit back and get an overall view. (I like to sit back literally and look at the Term Planning Calendar so I can easily see where several deadlines are on the same day or week.)

Looking at everything that is coming up will help you decide what is really an "H" and what is not. It need not cut into your social life, but it does mean that you may need to rearrange some things or say "no" to some invitations that come smack in the middle of your gathering data on gerbils.

But you can have fun and frolic on the nights and weekends that are far enough away from your "H" priorities. And, when personal "H" events come up (you really can't miss your sister's wedding no matter how much the gerbils need you), your Term Planning Calendar gives you enough warning so that you can make sure your school work doesn't suffer.

"I should have planned better"

Once you have a grasp of your obligations for a term at a time, bring the tasks down to the week at hand by filling out the Priority Tasks This Week form (see the sample on page 23). When planning study time for a test during the week, find the answers to these two questions: (1) "How much time do I *need* to devote to studying for this exam?" and (2) "How much time do I *have* to study for this exam?"

It's fairly easy to determine the answer to the second question. After all, there are a finite number of hours between now and the exam and you are filling in the "H" priorities and figuring that a certain amount of time devoted to sleeping and eating is necessary.

But the first question calls for a fairly definitive answer, too, or else you will never be able to plan.

Consider these other questions when figuring up the time needed:

- How much time do I usually spend studying for this type of exam? What have been the results? (If you usually spend three hours and you consistently get Ds, perhaps you need to think again.)

- What grade do I have going for me now? (If it's a solid B and you're convinced you can't get an A and you are content with a B, you may decide to devote less time to studying for the exam than if you have a C+ and an extra-good grade on the exam will give you a solid B. Just make sure you aren't overconfident and end up with an exam grade that will ruin your B forever.)

- What special studying do I have to do? (It's one thing to review notes and practice with a study group—more on that later in the book—but if you need to sit in a language lab and listen to hours of tapes or run the slower group of gerbils through the alphabet once more, plan your time accordingly.)

Priority Rating	Scheduled?	Priority Tasks This Week *Week of* ▨▨▨ *through* ▨▨▨

● Organize the materials you need to study, pace yourself and check to see how much material you have covered in the first hour of review. How does this compare to what you have left to study? Not every hour will be of equal merit (some hours, for whatever reason, will be more productive than others, while some material will take you longer to review), but you should be able to gauge pretty well from this first hour and from your previous experience.

I'll give you my Inverted Pyramid Theory in Chapter 4. It will show you how to plan the content of *what* you're reviewing so you get the maximum use out of your time.

Don't be dazed

Now we get to the Daily Schedule (see the sample on page 25), the piece of paper that will keep you sane as you move through the day.

Your Term Planning Calendar will most likely be on the wall beside your study area in your dorm, apartment or house. Your Priority Tasks This Week should be carried with you so that you can add any items that suddenly come up in class ("Oh," your teacher says, "did I forget to tell you that we have a quiz on Friday on the first two chapters?") or in conversation ("Go skiing with you this weekend? With you *and* your gorgeous twin? Let me check my calendar!").

And, of course, you'll carry your Daily Schedule so that you can be sure not to forget *anything*. The Daily Schedule, by the way, is divided into four categories:

1. **Assignments Due.** What has to be turned in on this day. Check before you leave for class. (This is like the "T" notations on my shopping list.)

Daily Schedule   *date:* [   ]

Assignments Due	Schedule
	5
	6
	7
	8
	9
To Do/Errands	10
	11
	12
	1
	2
	3
	4
	5
Homework	6
	7
	8
	9
	10
	11
	12

2. **To Do/Errands.** Don't depend on your memory. It's not that you can't remember; it's that you don't *need* to remember. This column will help you plan ahead (e.g., actually buying a birthday present before the birthday) and save you last-minute panics when you should be studying for the upcoming exam.

    As with any to-do list, make sure each item is really an item and not a combination of several steps (or stops). "Phone home" is one item; "arrange details for spring dance" is not.

3. **Homework.** When the teacher gives out homework assignments, here's where you can write them down so they're all together, complete with due dates, page numbers and any other information from the teacher.

4. **Schedule.** The actual list of events for the day from early morning to late at night. This is especially important when you have something extraordinary happening. For example, suppose that your teacher tells you to meet her in a different room for your 9:30 biology class. Again, if you depend on your memory alone, you will most likely be the only one who isn't getting to dissect a frog over in McGillicuddy Hall.

    In fact, you should highlight any unusual happenings like that with a brightly colored pen just to remind yourself. And take a moment to glance over the day's schedule *twice*: Look at it the night before, to psych yourself up for the coming day and make sure you didn't forget to do any special assignments. Then, glance at it again while you are having a quiet moment during your nutritious breakfast on the very day.

Examine schedule; schedule exam

Now that you have discovered the value of keeping track of upcoming events, including exams—and the possibility that you can actually plan ahead and keep your life from getting too crazy even during finals week—we can talk a little about the days prior to the exams themselves.

If you have an upcoming exam early in the morning and you are afraid you won't be in shape for it, do a bit of subterfuge on your body and brain.

Get up early for several days before the exam, have a good breakfast, and do homework or review your notes. This will help jump-start your body and brain and get used to the idea of having to solve equations or think seriously about the Punjab at an earlier-than-usual hour.

On the other end of the day, take care to get to bed early enough. Forego the late-night parties and the midnight movie on TV and actually devote enough time to getting some serious zzzzzs.

As time goes by

One last thing: Be honest with yourself. Don't block out two hours of study for your calculus exam *today* when you suspect your best friend will entice you to go with him to get a pizza and talk about anything *but* calculus. If you have budgeted six hours total to prepare for the exam, you've just cheated yourself out of a whole third of the time.

It's OK, in fact, to write down "pizza with Dave" for those two hours. Just be realistic and honest and budget your true study time when you will truly be studying.

Before you tackle Chapter 3, get those forms filled out. They will help you feel that your life actually is on the road from Chaos to Order. And—surprise, surprise—it's true!

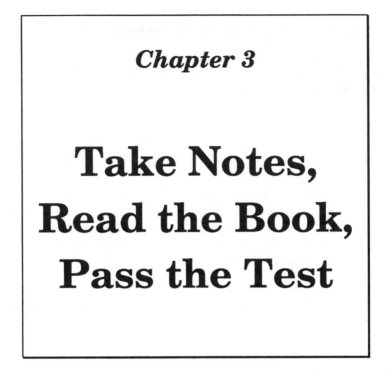

Chapter 3

Take Notes, Read the Book, Pass the Test

"He listens well who takes notes."
                            —Dante (1265-1321)

"Speaking of notes. As long as you're just sitting there, write your thank-you notes for your birthday gifts." —your mother

Once upon a time, there was a hard-working student named Melvin. He read his textbooks, took good notes in class, rarely missed a day of school, and always did his homework. Sitting next to him in class was a guy named

Steve. This guy *sort of* took notes, *kind of* read his textbook, and *usually* did his homework. Well, OK, not usually but *kind of* usually—if he came to class at all.

The day of the big test came. Hard-working Melvin got a D and slouchy, lazy Steve got an A....Not!

The first day of the test of your life

Well, maybe I shouldn't really say "test of your life." It sounds as if you may not come out of this one alive. Even the SAT isn't that important or scary!

What I really want to emphasize in this chapter was hinted at in the "once upon a time" story above: You don't start preparing for a test a couple of days before. You begin when you walk into the classroom on the first day—or even *before* that.

Everything you do in that course—attending every class, applying listening skills, taking good notes, doing your homework and reading all the assignments—helps you in "studying" for the exam.

Too many students think the exam is out there all by itself—floating out in space like a balloon that got loose from a bawling kid at a carnival. Nope. The role of the exam would be better described as a slice of pie with other "slices"—note taking, attendance, homework, etc.

For whom the alarm clock tolls

Yes, my friend, it may be cruel and it may be cold, but getting out of bed and going to class is the first step toward passing the final that's four months away.

"Oooh, missing that biology class just this one time can't huuuuurrrrrrt!" you moan as you roll over and bury your head under the pillow. "Why, oh why did I stay up so late?" you whine. "Why, oh why," you cry, "did I forget to iron something to wear?" "Why, oh why," you add, "was I ever born!"

Obviously, if this is you, you've got to start by getting to bed a little bit earlier, planning ahead a little bit more, and deciding that going to class is something you must do automatically.

Now that you're here...

All right. I've got you out of bed (and into a reasonably ironed outfit, I presume) and inside the classroom. You're awake, polite, respectful and listening. Now what?

Actually, that question needed to have been asked last night or several nights ago. You can't just waltz into class and be up to speed. When you arrive, you're expected by your teacher to have already accomplished the following:

1. You have read the assignment.
2. You have brought your notes/textbooks with you.
3. You have brought your homework assignment.
4. You have opened your notebook to the right page, opened the textbook to the current chapter and got out your homework to hand it in—all by the time the bell rings.

Is all of that cruel and inhuman punishment? Am I trying to make you into a student from a wildly competitive society somewhere along the Pacific Rim? No, I'm merely giving you a list of what will help you get the most out of the class—*long* before the test day arrives.

Pop goes the quiz

Not all tests, as you surely know by now, are announced. Your friendly neighborhood teacher may decide, out of malice, boredom or his lesson-plan book, to give you a pop quiz.

Now, how can you score well if you, first of all, aren't even in class and, second of all, haven't read the new material and periodically reviewed the old? And suppose it's an open-book test and you don't have a book to open?

Let's face it. Biology or U.S. history or economics or whatever 101 may not be your favorite subject but that doesn't mean you have to have an attitude about it. "Proving" you can't or won't do well in a class proves nothing.

Before that bell rings for class to begin, do all those things in the list on the previous page. Have your work ready to go so you don't waste time trying to find everything. Of course, if you've done a last-minute check back home or in the dorm, you'll know for sure that you've got the right books, notebooks, homework assignments, etc. Teachers get really tired of hearing, "I left it at home/in the car/in the dorm/ with my girl friend."

The next steps

Let's move on to what you should do during class, after class and before class.

First, during class, as we've already said, you need to listen. Not a difficult task, even when the teacher isn't going to win any elocution awards.

Teachers like to see students take notes. It shows them that you are interested in the topic at hand and that you think enough of what is being said to write it down. (And, if you've ever stood at the front of the room, you can usually tell who's taking notes and who's writing a letter to that friend in Iowa.)

Another of the books in this **HOW TO STUDY** *Program* is called *Take Notes*. As you can imagine, it goes into much more detail than I will here on taking good class notes. Let me deal, here, with *how* and *why* notes will help you study for—and pass—an exam.

First, a great deal of the material on most exams will come from your notes. A very good reason for never missing class. Even if you have to miss class (other students and the teacher would prefer that you remain home if you have a contagious tropical fever), you can get someone else's notes. On an occasional basis, this is OK. But you don't want to do this too often.

They are, after all, your friend's notes, not yours. Your friend has slightly different study habits, a slightly different body of knowledge to bring to class and different methods of concentration. He will not always write down things you would have because he knows them already or he was looking out the window at two squirrels playing touch football with a walnut. On the other hand, he will fill up half his pages with stuff that you would have skipped entirely because you know it's in detail on page 99.

You are your own best note-taker

I'm sure you've observed in your classes that some people are constantly taking notes. Others end up with two lines on one page. Most of us fall somewhere in between.

The person who never stops taking notes is either writing a letter to that friend in Iowa or has absolutely no idea what *is* or is *not* important.

The results are dozens of pages of notes (by the end of the semester) that may or may not be helpful. This person is so busy writing down stuff that he isn't prepared or even aware that he can ask and answer questions to help him understand the material better. To use that old adage, he can't see the forest for the trees. He is probably the same person who takes a marking pen and underlines or highlights every word in the book.

Contrast him to the person who thinks note-taking isn't cool, so he only writes down today's date and the homework assignment. He may write something when the teacher says, "Now, write this down and remember it," but he probably just scribbles some nonsense words. After all, he's cool.

Watch him sweat when it's time to study for the exam. He's stuck with a faulty memory and a textbook that may not contain half the material that will be on the test.

Notes: Tools of the trade

I found it very useful to type my notes after I'd written them in class. First of all, my handwriting won't win any prizes. (I noticed early on that very few people asked to borrow my notes. "Is this word 'Madagascar' or 'Muncie'?" they'd ask a little too loudly.)

Second, typing the notes gave me an opportunity to have a quick review of the class, spell out most of my abbreviations and—most importantly—discover if I missed anything. This gave me time to check my textbook or ask a classmate for the missing information. You don't want to discover this at midnight the night before the test.

A neater version of my notes was also extremely helpful when it came time to study for the test. I could read what was there, I had highlighted the most important elements, and the whole batch of notes just made more sense.

Looks aren't everything, but...

You'll want your class notes to be as readable and "study-able" as possible. Develop your own system of abbreviating words. In *Take Notes*, I provide you with a list of abbreviations that will help save you time. You will add many others as you become more familiar with the topics discussed in the class.

For example, if you're studying World War I, why write out the whole name of the war—ever? It's "WWI" or even "W" in your notes. When you type them up, you can still stick to this abbreviation.

Be consistent. Don't use "soc" one time for "sociology," and "soclgy" or "sogy" at other times, especially if some of your abbreviations for other words are close to any of these.

And, finally, when you are writing the notes in class, be consistent. If you put a dash or a dot in front of the first main point, then use the same system for the rest of them.

Reading is fundamental

Reading improves reading. In other words, if you hate reading or if you consider yourself a slow reader, keep at it anyway. Read anything and everything. Read at nights and on weekends. Read cereal boxes (even though the ingredients can be as scary as a Stephen King novel) and newspapers and magazines and short stories and....well, you get the idea.

As you may have guessed by now, or perhaps you already have looked in the front of this book, I also have a **HOW TO STUDY** book on this topic, too. It's called *Improve Your Reading* and, like the other books I've mentioned, it provides a lot of detail on how you can get more out of your reading.

Let's look at how you can use your reading skills—and improve them—to get higher grades. Here are some suggestions that help people read more efficiently:

1. When a chapter in a textbook has questions at the end, read the questions first. Why? They will give you an idea of what the chapter is all about and they will be "clues" as to what you should look for in the text.

2. Underline or highlight main points in the text. Don't, like our friend I mentioned earlier, mark too much or your efforts will be meaningless. At the same time, pay special attention to words and phrases the author has "highlighted" by placing them in italics or in boldface.

3. Don't skip over the maps, charts, graphs, photos or drawings. Much of this information may not also be in the text. If you skip it, you're skipping vital information.

4. What's the "big picture" here? We can get bogged down in the footnotes and unfamiliar words and lose touch with the purpose of the chapter. Review subheads, margin notes and questions and discussion points to get a grasp of the big picture.

5. Keep a balancing act between class discussions and notes, on the one hand, and the textbook (and any other workbooks) on the other. They will complement each other in their content. Let's suppose that you've read Chapter 8 already ("Japan and China in the 19th Century") and now you've discussed and taken notes on the same topic at least once in class.

   Sit down at your desk with both notes and Chapter 8 in front of you. Add information from the book to your notes but add it in this way: "10 reasons why opium trade flourished, pp. 112-113." Don't write down the 10 reasons since they are right there in the book, all neatly printed for you. But do this kind of cross-referencing so that you integrate the book with the notes.

6. Shortly before class, look over the chapter once again. Review what you and the author have decided are the most important points and mark

topics you want to ask the teacher to explain. (It's much better to have real questions rather than decide you're going to look smart by having a quota of questions each time. Teachers know the difference.)

The best time to study for your next class is right after the last one. Let's say you have Government 101 at 9:30 a.m. on Monday, Wednesday and Friday. As soon as you can after your Monday class, review that day's class notes, type them (if possible), and complete the reading assignment and other homework that's due on Wednesday.

Why? Because the class is fresh in your mind. Your notes are crying to be reviewed and corrected or added to, and you have a level of understanding that may not be there Tuesday night at 9 p.m.

Then, spend a little time on the same class and the same materials as close as possible to the next class. Let's say you can do that at 8:30 a.m. on Wednesday. The *big* study time is ASAP after Monday's class; the little *quick-let's-review* time comes shortly *before* Wednesday's class.

Now, let's refine these study habits for the next test. Follow me to Chapter 4, please.

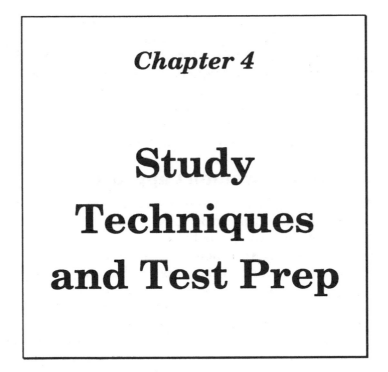

Chapter 4

Study Techniques and Test Prep

"You have to study a great deal to know a little."
—Charles de Secondat, Baron de Montesquieu
(1689-1755)

"Do you want to end up like your Uncle Harry? No? Then study!" —your mother

The baron thought he knew what he was talking about. And he did, but he said that in the days before books like the one you're holding were written. I'm going to be so bold as to amend what he said: "You have to study a reasonable amount to know a great deal."

Why change his centuries-old words? Because we know a lot about study techniques that he didn't. We also have the advantage of a lot of modern conveniences (I'm talking about such things as language labs, not MTV). And because we can concentrate on studying *smarter*, not harder.

Enough baron-bashing. Let's look at how we can study "a reasonable amount" and do well on the exams that are intended to find out if we know what we think we do.

The pharaohs wouldn't approve

Now I'll tell you about the Inverted Pyramid Theory I mentioned earlier in the book.

The top is very wide, the bottom is very narrow. This is symbolic of the way you should study for a test. Begin with all possible materials (all notes, book chapters, workbooks, audio tapes, etc.) and briefly review everything to see what you need to spend time with and what you can put aside.

I also call this separating the wheat from the chaff. The wheat is the edible good stuff that's taken from the field and turned into Chocolate Sugar Munchies. The chaff stays behind. The chaff was important at one time but it no longer is needed. The same is true of some of your material you've gathered for this next test. Now try this:

1. Gather all the material you have been using for the course: books, workbooks, hand-outs, notes, homework, previous tests and papers.
2. Compare the contents with the material you will be tested on and ask yourself: What exactly do I need to review for this test?
3. Select the material for review. Reducing the pile of books and papers will be a psychological aid— suddenly, it seems as if you will have enough time and energy to study for the test.

4. Photocopy and complete the Pre-Test Organizer on page 90. Consider carefully the "Material to be covered" section on the second page.

   Be specific. The more detailed you are, the better job you'll do in reviewing all the areas that you should know. This exercise will help you *quantify* what you need to do. Instead of wandering aimlessly through your materials, you will have told yourself just where this information is.

5. As you review the material and conclude that you know it for the test, put a bold check mark on the "OK" line. You are, to use my example, inverting the pyramid or shrinking the amount of material you need to study.

   And you have time not only to spend on the stuff that's giving you grief, but to seek out other sources (fellow students, the teacher, the library, etc.) and get to the heart of the matter.

6. By the time the test is given, you should have reduced the "pyramid" to nothing. Go into the test and do well!

Skim and scan, skim and scan

You neither have time nor a valid reason to reread all the material. You *do* need to skim and scan it to pull out the essence and remind yourself of the main points.

Skimming is reading fast for an overview, for general information. Scanning is reading fast to find specifics. Both emphasize "fast" and "reading." You don't flip the pages of the book so quickly that you get a chill from the breeze. But you don't start reading the book all over again either.

Look at what you've underlined and highlighted. Look at boldfaced and italicized words, subheads, captions, questions—all in all, the "meat" of the chapter.

You're going to use the same reading methods with the other study material, including your notes. Probably your notes, however, should receive the most careful attention since they will reflect the teacher's lectures and her viewpoints and biases, as well as key buzzwords.

You don't want to obsess on your notes, but you can make notes from your notes as you study for the test. What I like to do is pull out of the notes the central ideas of the material being tested, sort of getting the *super*wheat out of the wheat.

The way of all flash

You probably remember flash cards from elementary school. On one side was a picture, on the other a word. Or one side held a definition ("Someone who studies bugs"), and the other the word being defined ("entomologist").

Flash cards are one of my favorite ways to test myself. They also work well with two people studying together or with a group. They work well for studying vocabulary, short answers, definitions, matching ("Boise" and "potato"), even true and false.

No person is an island

Don't face the Huguenots alone. Or even the periodic table of the elements. Share *your* knowledge while you benefit from the knowledge of a handful of other students in the same class. In other words, form a study group.

Try, if you can, to study with others who are at your level or slightly above. I say, *slightly* above. If you're a solid C and they're easy-A people, you won't connect. You'll want to review information they'll agree to skip. (And the opposite will happen to *you* if you choose people too far below you.)

Study groups are valuable as long as you also keep a fair amount of time set aside to work on your own. After all, you have to know this stuff by yourself to take the exam.

Keep the group serious. Sure, pizza and gossip can be great combinations, but not when you have budgeted two hours to review for the English final.

Keep the group small. There is little merit in more than four or five people getting together. If the group is too big, the natural talkers and leaders and bosses will take over (although they are not necessarily the natural *best* or most helpful students in the group) and the smart, shy ones will hide behind the couch.

Don't meet too often. A very few, short meetings will give you an intensity and seriousness that you need. Also, you need to work on your own between the meetings, and you'll need some time for that.

Come to the group with questions on areas you don't understand. Bring your notes, textbook and workbooks with you so you can settle disputes and use them for references when others are asking their questions.

Previews of coming attractions

Use the combined smarts of the group to come up with a reasonable facsimile of the approaching test. Divide up the assignments so each of you writes the questions (and can prove the answers) to one section.

Work through this test at your next group meeting. The person who wrote the section should lead the discussion. This is not the time to play "I'll answer first and show how smart I am." Keep friends from yelling out the answers. Use this time, instead, to discuss why the correct answer is correct and why the other choices *aren't* so that all of you— not just Bob Bigmouth—really understand what's going down.

41

Play it again, Mr. Sam

If you have access to old exams written by the same teacher, especially if they cover the same material you're going to be tested on, use them also for review.

Chances are the very same questions will *not* appear again. But the way the test is prepared, the kinds of questions, the emphasis on one kind of question over another (100 true/false, 50 multiple-choice and one—count 'em—one essay), will give you clues to what your own test will be about. At the same time, see if you can find anyone who had this teacher for this class last year or last semester. Can they give you any advice, tips, hints or warnings?

Mnemonics and other words

What is that word, anyway? It refers to the practice of reducing a list of things you have to know to a simple way to remember them for the test. Warning: Some of these may stick with you for life. Here's an example:

Let's say you have to memorize the Seven Deadly Sins. (I said memorize them, not practice them.) I know—if you have one more list to learn, you'll scream. So make it a game, and make it easy to remember for the test.

"Sloth" is one of the seven. Think of lying around the house, having breakfast with a friend (instead of taking tests, going to class and all that). "Eggs pal" is your answer. The letters stand for the seven sins: In order, they are envy, greed, gluttony, sloth, pride, anger and lust.

You can also get pretty silly by making up associations that will help you remember a list of items or several matching pairs. It's more fun—and probably more successful—than memorizing long lists of facts for those times that you just need to know the information but you won't be needing it for the rest of your life.

An example of an association would be as follows: "I cry 'cause you gonna go, and Low Mate go to a free town with sarah alone." (Put a calypso beat to it.)

This beautifully crafted sentence contains clues to the answer to the following: "Match the following African countries with their capital cities."

Ghana	Freetown
Togo	Accra
Sierra Leone	Lome

Yes, of course, it's reaching. That's how associations work.

But suppose you couldn't remember which city went with which country. Or which political movement went with which social reformer. Or whatever. Use a "silly" way to hold the information together for you long enough for you to avoid a "silly" grade on the test.

Outsmarting Weird Al Teachovic

In an ideal world, all teachers would be filled with knowledge they eagerly and expertly shared with their students. Their lectures would be exciting (and brief). And their tests would be fair and accurate measurements of what the students should have learned.

Before you tell me about pigs flying, let me say that, in spite of the criticism schools and teachers have been getting for years, there are a lot of teachers out there like that. If you don't think you've had one yet, your turn is coming up.

In the meantime, though, let's consider Weird Al (or Weird Alice.) His personality may come out, unfortunately, when he writes and grades his tests. If you're lucky, you'll be forewarned by his former students so that you can be prepared as much as possible.

Watch for these danger signs. Even if he never seems to know when the next test will be, try to get that answer out of him. (Believe me, you want to ask. It's better to discover that it's a week from Thursday *today* rather than finding out a week from Wednesday.)

If he says he doesn't know what the test will cover, keep asking him. Also ask what types of questions will be on the test (true/false, multiple choice, essays, etc.) and what percentage of the test will be devoted to each. By your questions, you are helping him shape the test in his mind, and giving him the information he needs to give back to you.

Once you've taken the test, check your corrected test paper carefully. (This is true in any course, but here it's even more important.) If a right answer was marked wrong, let him know. If the question is too ambiguous and your answer could be right as well as the one *he* says is right, let him know.

And now, h-e-e-e-e-r-r-e-e-e's the SAT!

Well, you did it. You registered to take the SAT and the Day of Reckoning is approaching.

While I'll share some specifics on taking any test, including the SAT, in the next few chapters, for right now just remember that any hours-long national standardized test requires a lot of the same skills and the same planning as any unit quiz, chapter test, mid-term or final.

Since the SAT is intended to test your general knowledge of many areas, rather than grill you on the details from Chapter 14 of your chemistry book, you can and you *cannot* study for it. You cannot study specific material. On the other hand, you have been studying for the SAT all your life. (Jeez, now that sounds scary!)

This test will seek to find out what you know about a lot of different subjects. Some of the answers will come from knowledge you gained years before. Other will come from your ability to work out the problems right there, using techniques and knowledge you gained years ago—and some you gained only this semester.

To prepare for the SAT, I have one big suggestion: Determine, based on your past test-taking experiences and your comfort levels, what your weak areas are. Do you continually and completely mess up essay questions? Do analogies spin you out of control? Do you freeze at the sight of an isosceles triangle?

Seek out teachers, librarians and school counselors who can guide you to samples of these kinds of questions. Ask your teachers and fellow students for advice on handling the areas you feel you are weak in, take the sample tests, then work on evaluating how you did. Keep testing yourself and keep evaluating how you are doing.

Get advice from students who say things like, "Analogies? Piece of cake!" Find out if they really can do them easily and get tips from them (and from what I say in the following chapters).

Also, a good, solid review of basic math and English will be valuable. If geometry is not your strong suit, find a book that contains lists of the fundamentals and spend time reviewing information that you will be expected to exercise on the SAT. Do the same with the other subject areas to be tested. If your library doesn't have such materials, get advice from teachers or from the counseling office.

To be coached or not to be coached?

Should you take one of those SAT preparation courses everyone's talking about? Is it worth the money, the time, the effort, the bother, when you've got so many other important things looming in your life, like the party on Saturday, the party on Sunday and the party on Monday?

The answer is a definite "maybe." It depends on a handful of factors: First of all, ask others for recommendations. Listen closely to why they liked or disliked a particular course (their reasons may not match your reasons—tread carefully here).

Decide if you have the time and money to take a course. If you do, which kind do you want? There are coaching classes taught by humans, but there are also books/cassette tapes combos and computer programs. Ask your school counseling office for recommendations, also. (They may even have copies of some of the programs.)

There's method in their madness—I think

The SAT coaching programs should deal with two areas. I'll call them Method and Content.

Method is the study of *how* to take a test, specifically how to take the SAT. That portion of the course will cover much of the same material that you're reading in this book, especially the material we're going to look at in the next two chapters.

Content deals with practicing the sort of stuff that's going to be on the SAT: vocabulary words, math problems, essay questions, analogies and so on.

The two areas overlap, of course. When you work math problems there are "methods" you utilize to get the answer, just as there is "content."

Practicing for the SAT by answering questions that are similar in content to what you will later be tested on is a very valuable exercise, but it's only half the equation. The other half is the feedback you get from your coach (or favorite teacher, counselor, or fellow students) on how you did, what you did, and why you did what you did. It won't do you any good to keep messing up on analogies, for example, if you can't stop and figure out how to do them right.

The "write" way to do the *new* SAT

The new SAT is coming. And it's going to require you to do more writing than your elders have done in recent years.

The revised SAT will consist of two major components: the SAT-I: Reasoning Tests, and the SAT-II: Subject Tests.

The first group of students to take the SAT-I will be the venerable Class of '95 after its introduction in 1994. The SAT-II has already begun seeping under the door.

They laughed when I SAT at the piano

Your school counselor can give you details on the changes that will be taking place, but here's a quick summary of the SAT-I for those of you younger than the Class of '95:

1. Revised and expanded versions of the verbal and math tests that are in the current SAT.

2. Longer reading passages that will measure critical reading skills (in fact, questions on critical reading will make up at least half the new verbal test).

3. Most of the verbal test time will be spent on reading passages and questions to test your ability to interpret, synthesize, analyze and evaluate what you're reading.

4. You will be tested on vocabulary in context (vocabulary will appear in sentences, phrases, paragraphs and passages rather than in a long word list).

5. Antonyms will be dropped (guess they weren't popular enough), but sentence completions and analogies will remain.

6. The math test will ask you to produce your own answers for some of the questions rather than just select answers from a list of choices. You will also be able to use a calculator (yeahhhh!).

The SAT-II will include a brand-new test where students write an impromptu essay on an assigned topic and answer questions on usage, sentence structure and paragraph revision.

What's up between now and 1994

Actually, one of the changes has already taken place. In June 1991, the new Mathematics Level IIC was inaugurated. ("C" stands for "calculator"—be sure the one you use is "approved" or you'll be thrashed, beaten and refused admission to the test.)

This test covers topics such as coordinate geometry in two or three dimensions, transformations and solid geometry. It places emphasis on properties and graphs of the trigonometric functions, the inverse trigonometric functions, trigonometric equations and identities, and the laws of sines and cosines. Whew!

Chapter 5

Essays: Go for Quality, Not Quantity

"There is no room for the impurities of literature in an essay." —Virginia Woolf (1882-1941)

"Essay: ...an irregular indigested piece." —Samuel Johnson (1709-1784)

Just be glad that dear Virginia isn't grading your SAT.

Essay questions. Some students love them. Some hate them. It's hard to feel indifferent about those lengthy sections that can take up pages and pages of a test—and pages and pages of an answer booklet.

Write on!

Really advanced schools with big budgets provide type-writers or computers for their students so they can write essays in the classroom. But we can't all have 90210 as our ZIP code. The rest of you will have to work with a pen.

First of all, make sure it's a pen. And a good one. One that you're comfortable with. If you hate ballpoints and swear by felt-tipped pens, then go for it. Actually, go for *them*. Only someone who wants a really bad grade shows up with one pen. Of course, it will run out, begin to leak, break or all of the above if you have only one. If you have two (or, for the truly superstitious, three or more) then, of course, the first pen will be working like that annoying drum-beating rabbit when your grandchildren are taking the SAT on Mars.

Pause your paw

Don't ever, *ever* begin writing the answer to an essay question without a little "homework" first. I don't care if you're the school's prize-winning journalist.

First, really look at the question. Are you sure you know what it's asking? What are the verbs? Don't "describe" when it calls for you to "compare and contrast." Don't "explain" when it tells you to "argue." Underline the verbs.

Then sit back a minute and think about what you're going to say. Or less than a minute, depending on how much time you have, but *don't* just start writing.

The second task to perform before you start writing is to make an outline. Not one with Roman numerals—this outline will consist of a simple list of abbreviated words, scribbled on a piece of scrap paper or in the margin of your test booklet. The purpose of this outline is the same as those fancy ones: to make sure you include everything you need and want to say—in order.

Let's suppose this is the essay question: "Discuss the effects of Mabel Dodge Luhan on the cultural and social life of Taos, New Mexico." Your outline might look like this:

1. intro   —ovrvw MDL on T
           —brt a&w, stay

2. social —top dog
           —salon
           —a&w brt a&w
           —a. scene

3. cult.   —hist. Sp/NA
           —hse/gr

4. conc.   —wht lke?
           —thks her
           —incr.

Notice that almost no words are written out completely. After all, no one is going to grade this outline. In fact, no one else is even going to *see* it. Let me write out the whole outline for you. You won't do this, of course, but I want you to see, before you read the actual essay, what I had in mind when I wrote out those hieroglyphics above.

1. Introduction
    A. Overview of Mabel Dodge Luhan's influence on Taos.
    B. She brought artists and writers to visit and that some of them moved there.

2. Social effects
    A. Mabel was the head of "society" in Taos.
    B. She created a "salon" atmosphere in her home.

   C. Her friends, the famous artists and writers, brought other artists and writers to Taos—and to Mabel.

3. Cultural effects
   A. Historic aspects, especially the promotion of the Native American and Spanish cultures.
   B. Her own house and grave today are part of the historic/cultural scene.

4. Conclusion
   A. Taos wouldn't be the same without her.
   B. Thanks to her, it's a bustling town today filled with artistic residents and visitors.
   C. The cultural and social scene—which she developed—continues to increase in numbers and importance.

You are going to start off strong, with bold statements that begin the discussion and refer directly to the question. This introduction will put Mabel in context.

In this second part of the outline ("social effects"), you begin to deal with the gut issue of the essay. There have been whole books written about Mabel, so you aren't going to be able to tell everything about her in one comparatively short essay. Nor, more importantly, should you. The question, after all, doesn't say, "Tell as much as you can cram into one blue book about Mabel Dodge Luhan." No, it asks for specific, limited, restricted and definite answers.

I might as well make my "quality, not quantity" speech here, too. I hope you write well. It's important. But excellent writing, even pages and pages of it, will not get you an excellent grade unless you have the quality—hard-hitting, incisive, direct answers.

Again, most teachers won't fall for the beautifully crafted, empty answer. Don't depend on your good looks or your command of the subjunctive to get you by. Go home and study.

But, back to the second item on your outline. You will write about the social effects—one-half of the question, at this point. Give examples and be as specific as you can. If the teacher has provided certain information that you dutifully copied into your notes, be sure to include this information here. If the teacher was really enthusiastic about something and referred to it a number of times, take the hint—and take your pen and give that information back in your own words.

Think of the introduction and the conclusion as the bread in a sandwich, with the information in between as the hamburger, lettuce, tomato and pickle. Everything is necessary for it all to hang together, but the main attraction is going to be what's between the slices.

Now, let's see how I'd write this essay:

The Effects of Mabel Dodge Luhan on the Cultural and Social Life of Taos, New Mexico

Mabel Dodge Luhan had an extraordinary effect on the life of the little mountain town of Taos, New Mexico. From the time she arrived in 1917 until her death in 1962, Mabel was the social and cultural life of the town. She not only brought her own personality to the artists' colony, but numerous artists and writers to visit Taos as well. Some of them remained in the area for the rest of their lives.

The gatherings of these famous people—D.H. Lawrence, Georgia O'Keeffe, Greta Garbo, Leopold Stokowski and others—in Mabel's house served as a kind of "salon" where important members of the American and European artistic communities met, discussed each other's work, and spread the word about Taos and Mabel when they returned to New York, California or Europe. Their enthusiasm helped bring even more famous people to visit Taos.

The social scene in Taos centered on Mabel. Because she was a personal friend of most of the people who visited her, as well as being wealthy, domineering and extremely active, she reigned as the head of the social order in the town during her entire lifetime. The other prominent members of the community—the artists, the wealthy ranchers, the merchants—all formed a pecking order beneath her.

Mabel's support of the artistic community earlier in this century helped spread the fame of these artists—and increased the sale of their works. The prominence of Taos as an artists' colony, thanks in part to Mabel, encouraged even more artists to move to Taos, which, in turn, increased the number of visitors who came to town to buy art or simply to look at it—while spending money at the restaurants, hotels, bars and gift shops. This trend has continued—Taos today is a major art center in the U.S. with dozens of art galleries and tourist-related shops.

The historic, as well as artistic, aspects of Taos were promoted by Mabel. Her artist friends painted people, places and events connected to the local Spanish and Native American cultures. These paintings, and the media attention given to the historic aspects of the town, helped spread the fame of Taos.

Today, Mabel's house and her grave, in the historic Kit Carson Cemetery, are two of many attractions that tourists visit when they come to town.

It is difficult to imagine what Taos would be like today had Mabel Dodge Luhan not taken up residence there in 1917. For 45 years, her promotion of the little town gave it worldwide fame. Artists, historians, writers and tourists began to visit Taos. Each year, the number of visitors—and social and cultural events, art galleries and historic tours—increases, thanks to the influence of Mabel Dodge Luhan.

There. You may never write about Mabel (all of the above is true, by the way), but if you "translate" the outline/essay exercise to a topic you are studying (the French Revolution, Chicago architecture or the influence of the hot dog on National League batting averages), you can do the same.

Give me some space, man

Plan ahead. Write your essay on every other line and on one side of the paper or page only. This will give you room to add or correct anything without having to write it so small that it is illegible and, therefore, doesn't earn you any credit. It also helps keep the whole paper neater and, psychologically, that should help you get a slightly better grade. Most teachers won't admit it, but they will give a few more points to tests that are neat, clean and done with a good pen. Think about it. How many slobs do you know who are "A" students?

Proof it!

Budget your time so that you can go back over your essay, slowly, and correct any mistakes or make any additions. Check your spelling, punctuation, grammar and syntax. (And if you don't know what that is, find out. You'll need to know for the SAT.) It would be a shame for you to write a beautiful essay and lose points because you had those kinds of errors.

When you're done, you're done...almost

Resist the temptation to leave the room or turn in your paper before you absolutely have to. Imagine the pain of sitting in the cafeteria, while everyone else is back in the room, continuing to work on the test, and you suddenly remember what else you could have said to make your essay really sparkle. But it's too late!

Take the time at the end of the test to review not only your essay answers, but your other answers as well. Make sure all words and numbers are readable. Make sure you have matched the right question and the right answer. Even make sure you didn't miss a whole section by turning over a page too quickly. Make sure you can't, simply *can't*, add anything more to any of the essay answers. Make sure. Make sure. Make sure.

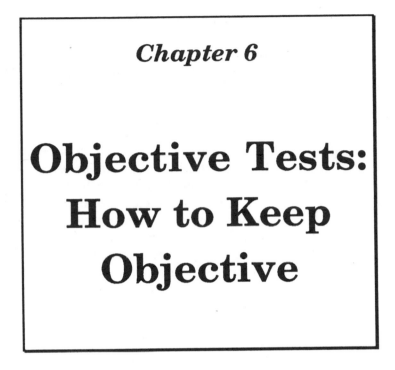

Chapter 6

Objective Tests: How to Keep Objective

"You want me to be objective? OK, I'll be objective. (A) Clean your room. (B) Take out the trash. (C) Sweep the walk. (D) Do all of the above. The answer, I'll tell you straight away, is (D)." —your mother

Unlike your mother, the test isn't going to give you the answer right there and then. Except that, in multiple-choice questions, the answer is staring you in the face (and sticking out its tongue at you, if you want to know the truth). You just have to be able to figure out which one it is.

In this chapter, we're going to look at the different types of objective questions and some of the methods to use to answer each type, based primarily on something called "the process of elimination."

If you learn nothing else from this chapter, learn this: The process of elimination has saved many a person from failure. Learn to use it.

Your guess genes

Should you or shouldn't you guess on an objective test? We didn't bring this up in the last chapter on essay tests because it's pretty hard to "guess" when you haven't a clue what to write about. You may have clues to answering objective questions, however. I'm going to show you some.

But back to the question about guessing. You can't answer the question unless you ask the teacher a couple more questions. First, what are the penalties for guessing? If he doesn't take off any points for guessing, then guess away. You'd be foolish to leave a single answer blank.

I hope you won't have to do it so haphazardly, of course, and so do you. But when there is a zero percent chance of getting any points for the question if you leave it blank—and a 25 percent chance if you put *any* answer down, don't hesitate to do that.

Guessing when it won't hurt you in the least is the easy decision. What if, however, the teacher says that each correct answer in Section III is worth two points, each incorrect answer will mean you get one point deducted, and no answer at all (leaving it blank) means you get no points added or subtracted.

Take a moment here to reflect on this. You are taking a risk if you guess, especially if you make a wild stab. This is where the process of elimination comes into play, along with "educated" guessing. (They're sort of the same thing—we could say that the process of elimination allows you to make an educated guess.)

Eliminate the obvious and sort-of obvious

Suppose the question was as follows: "The first U.S. President to appoint a woman to the Cabinet was (A) Franklin D. Roosevelt, (B) Herbert Hoover, (C) Abraham Lincoln or (D) Jimmy Carter."

Heck if I know, you may be saying. Most likely, you can get this down to two choices pretty quickly. Why? Think about women's rights and the role of women in society. OK, that's long enough.

You're absolutely correct to eliminate, right away, Abraham Lincoln. It wasn't that he was a bad guy; you just have to remember that women didn't even have the right to vote at that time, and laws and customs kept women from doing most of what they are doing today. The likelihood of a woman being in the President's Cabinet in the 1860s is very, very, very slim.

Let's now go to the other extreme. You may be fuzzy on who was in Jimmy Carter's Cabinet (he may have been fuzzy, too), but even if you are too young to remember Carter, you're guessing that he was recent enough not to be the first president to appoint women in that role. Score another point for the process of elimination.

Now comes the hard part. If you have any knowledge of history, and I hope you do, you know that the two remaining choices were, at least, presidents during the 20th century...in other words, after women got the right to vote. (Women could have served in the Cabinet without the right to vote, but it isn't very logical, is it? That's why I'm pegging my answer to that historic decision.)

You may not be able to get past this choice. But, even if you can't, and you blindly select one or the other, your chance of selecting the correct answer is one out of two. Even if your teacher deducts points, I would go ahead and put down (A) or (B).

Those of you who know a little more about history than average are going to be able to figure it out by remembering that Roosevelt was a very different sort of President. He was loved or hated for his dramatic changes in government, while Hoover was the poster boy for The Status Quo Society. If that difference in their styles and actions comes to mind, then you'd be 100 percent correct to choose FDR.

Check it out, check it out!

Use this process of elimination for all types of objective questions. Depending on whether you can eliminate any of the answers and whether you feel you can "afford" to lose the points will help you decide how to answer the question.

If there is time during a test for you to come back to questions and look at them one more time, go ahead and put a line through the answers you know can't be correct. That will simply save you time. You will ignore the answers that are struck out and concentrate on the ones that remain. A small point, but it can save you several seconds.

Get visual

Throughout a test, don't miss an opportunity to draw a picture for yourself if this will help you understand the question and figure out the right answer.

I believe in being as visual as possible. If the question deals with any sort of cause-and-effect that has several steps in it, literally draw or write down those steps very quickly, using abbreviated words or symbols. It's like making a quick outline, as we discussed in the chapter on essay questions.

Putting it down like that may help you see any missing pieces, help you understand relationships between any of the parts and, thus, help you select the right answer.

And the answer is...!

Especially with multiple-choice answers, read the question, then try to guess the answer before you look at what's there. Very often, you'll be right—or at least you'll be close and you can begin the elimination process immediately.

12 tips for "Acing" multiple-choice tests

1. Be careful you don't read too much into questions. You can try to second-guess the test preparer, get too elaborate and ruin the answer.
2. Underline the key words.
3. If two choices are very similar, the answer is probably not either one of them.
4. If two choices are opposite, one of them is probably correct.
5. Don't go against your first impulse unless you are *sure* you were wrong. (Sometimes you're so smart you scare yourself.)
6. Check for negatives and other words that are there to throw you off. ("Which of the following is *not*....")
7. The answer is usually wrong if it contains "all, always, never or none." Usually.
8. The answer has a great chance of being right if it has "sometimes, probably or some."
9. When you don't know the right answer, look for the wrong one. Start *that* process rolling.
10. Don't eliminate an answer unless you actually know what every word means.
11. Read every answer (unless you are wildly guessing at the last minute and there's no penalty).
12. If it's a standardized test, consider transferring all the answers from one section to the answer

sheet at the same time. This can save time. Just be careful: make sure you're putting each answer in the right place.

Analogies: Study/Succeed as Eat/Live

Analogies are to objective tests as "Don't even think of leaving this house without a coat" is to your mother.

I may be a sick puppy, but I like analogies. In the heat of completing 30 of them on a test, I may have slight second thoughts, but I look upon them as incredible brain teasers.

Pause with me a minute while I practice a little pop psychology. Think of any of these tests, even the SAT, as a game. I don't mean you don't take it seriously. But you want to get the highest score or the best grade possible.

But look upon it as you might a sports event. It's a challenge. You've prepared mentally just as you would prepare physically for basketball or tennis. Why not look upon it in a positive sense, as a challenge for you to take on, to compete with yourself for the best possible outcome?

If you have that kind of attitude, you will remain in a better frame of mind prior to the test and during it, and you'll do better. End of sermon. Back to analogies.

Taking it all apart

To help you figure out the right answer in an analogy, write it out, or, at least, think it out. Suppose the question was as follows:

POLICE: ARREST
    (A) priest: church
    (B) doctor: prescribe
    (C) driver: sleep
    (D) lawyer: court

Begin by deciding what the relationship is between "police" and "arrest." First of all, what parts of speech are "police" and "arrest" in this example? If you're not suffering from too much heavy-metal music appreciation, you should come up with "noun: verb."

The correct answer is going to have the same relationship. Two of the answers, (B) and (C), are noun: verb. For "priest" to be considered, it would have to be something like "priest: pray" or "priest: preach." Likewise, (D) would have to be something like "lawyer: practice" or "lawyer: sue" to have the same relationship of the parts of speech.

So we've eliminated two of the four already. Look at the police example. What is the relationship between "police" and "arrest?" If you write or think it out, you'll come up with: "arrest is one thing police do as part of their job."

Which now seems correct? The doctor or the driver? If you substitute "doctor" and "prescribe" in the above sentence, doesn't that sound correct? But if you put "driver" and "sleep" in the same places, does it make sense? Not really. We assume that, at some point or other, all drivers sleep (at least we hope so as they are rapidly maneuvering us through traffic on the way home from school), but it isn't a part of their job.

Some samples for you to taste

Many of these basic principles apply to the other types of questions you'll find on an objective test. Matching one item with another, completing sentences, doing math problems, choosing the correct vocabulary word—all rely on:

1. (a) your prior knowledge gained from studying for this particular course

   (b) all the reading, studying and listening you've been doing for years

2. your common sense
3. your ability to eliminate as many as possible of
   the potential answers
4. paying close attention to and following directions

Let's run through an example of another type of question, this one involving antonyms:

MAMMOTH: (A) colossal
              (B) minuscule
              (C) perpendicular
              (D) moderate

The test-writer has thrown in (A) to see if you'll flub up and choose a synonym instead. Not exactly dirty pool, but a technique to watch for. And (C) is there as a kind of off-center joke. Huh? But some people think that, because it is so unusual, it must be right.

Answer (D) is a variation on (A) in that it refers to size, but it's not the right size for the answer.

The correct answer must be (B), and it is. Even if you didn't know what "minuscule" meant, you should have been able to figure out that "mini" is tiny or little or as close to the opposite of "mammoth" as you're going to get here.

Comprehension questions

This is the portion of the test where you find a short essay, followed by several questions. You are supposed to find the answers to those questions in the essay.

Unlike the multiple-choice questions, where the answer is actually right in front of you, the answers to the essay questions may well be hidden in one fashion or another.

Not since third grade have you had an essay question that asks, "How old was Thomas Jefferson when he first went to Bloomingdale's?" and, lo and behold, back in the essay it clearly says, "Thomas Jefferson was 17 when he visited Bloomingdale's for the first time." Unfortunately for you, those questions went out with notes that said, "Do you love me? Yes or No!," and recess.

You're lucky if you get questions like, "How old was Thomas Jefferson when he became President?" and the essay says, "Thomas Jefferson ascended to the office of the President 33 years after his first election as a member of the Virginia House of Burgesses in 1768."

Buried somewhere else in the essay will be something like, "Jefferson, born 33 years before the Declaration of Independence, ..." Since you should know that the Declaration of Independence was written in 1776, you can figure out he was born in 1743 and that he became President in 1801. The rest is history.

Don't confuse me with facts

Look at that example again. Did it ever say the year of Jefferson's birth or the year he became President? Nope. It gave you, in two different places, enough information to figure it out.

At the same time, those terrible tricksters have thrown in enough dates and enough numbers to get people to write down "33" or "66" as the right answer. Also, they don't offer the information in strict chronological order—another way to mess you up.

This is where too little attention to detail can get a wrong answer on paper. Before you search for the answer, you need to decide what the question is.

Don't jump to conclusions so quickly that you grab the first number that you see. In fact, you can be pretty sure that any number that you see will *not* be the answer.

"Ace" Any Test

In the Jefferson example, you might have quickly scribbled down the following information just to get your bearings, and the correct answer:

1. 1776	2. 1768	3. 1801
- 33	+ 33	-1743
1743 birth	1801 Prez	58

Here's the method I recommend for answering comprehension questions:

1. Read the questions first. Consider them clues in a puzzle. You'll be alerted to what the essay is about so that you don't start "cold" with the first paragraph.
2. Slowly read the essay, keeping in mind the questions you've just read. Don't underline too much, but do underline conjunctions that change the direction of the sentence: however, although, nevertheless, yet, etc. Because of this shift, there is a good chance that this sentence will figure in one of the questions.

   For example, this sentence in the essay, "John Smith was the kind of writer who preferred writing over editing, *while* his wife Lois was interested in the latter over the former," might provide the answer to the question: "Did Lois Smith prefer writing or editing?" A too-careless glance back at the text will cause you to select "writing" as the answer.
3. Read the questions again. Then go back and forth, finding out the answer to the first one, the second one, etc. Don't skip around unless the first question is an absolute stumper. If you jump around too much, you'll get confused again and

you won't answer any of the questions very completely or even correctly.

Matching

Match the following countries with their capitals:

Thailand	Paris
Kenya	
Japan	Tokyo
Turkey	
France	Kuala Lumpur
India	
Malaysia	Bangkok

Match the obvious ones first. Let's say you know Paris and Tokyo are the capitals of France and Japan, respectively. Look at the two remaining ones. Here's where common sense and good general knowledge will come in handy.

Because you probably get a lot of your world news from the radio and TV, you may well have heard the combos more than you've seen them. Go with the ones that "sound right." (In this case, Bangkok, Thailand and Kuala Lumpur, Malaysia.)

Multiple-choice math

Process of elimination is important in finding the answers. There are some numbers to consider, also. For example, scan the problem below and see if you can figure out the answer without actually doing the math:

$334 \times 412 =$	(A)	54,559
	(B)	137,608
	(C)	22,528
	(D)	229,766

By performing one simple task, you can eliminate two of the possible answers. Multiply the last digits in each number (2 x 4). The answer must end in 8.

Now, eyeball (B) and (C). Can you find the right answer quickly? Here you are doing educated guessing known in math circles as "guesstimating." Look: 334 x 100 is 33,400. You should be able to do that without any tools. Therefore, (C) has to be wrong. You are left with (B).

Should you do the actual math to double-check your answer? I wouldn't. You know that (A) and (D) are wrong. Absolutely. You know from a quick ballpark multiplying that (C) is much too low. Mark (B) as the answer and move on.

Sentence completions

Like many of the other kinds of problems, sentence completions can often be figured out by putting the question into context or into perspective. Here's an example:

"The hypnotist said to the man, 'You're very _____.'"

    (A) sleepy   (D) ill
    (B) rich   (E) busy
    (C) ugly

Quick. What do hypnotists do? What do they say (at least in the movies)? It has to be (A). Now, somewhere since the dawn of time, a hypnotist has said all of the other words. He may also have said, "Do you know what Spiro Agnew's doing now?" but that doesn't make the words right. We're looking for logic and common sense here.

Vocabulary

The best way to do well on this section of the test is to *have* a large vocabulary. Hey, what a great piece of advice, you're saying. But it's true.

Large vocabularies come from a lot of reading and a lot of listening. And I don't mean listening to Madonna. A good working vocabulary will also help you in every other section of every other test since you are more likely to understand the directions, the questions and the possible answers.

What can I say? Build your vocabulary as much as you can. Read good books. Listen to people with large vocabularies. Write down the words you don't know and become friendly with them. The more words you know, the better you can play the "process of elimination" game and the better score you'll get.

All of the above, none of the above

Some teachers have fallen in love with "all of the above" and "none of the above." You can't take one of their tests without those phrases appearing in every other question. Just a word of caution: Before you can select "all," you must be positive that all the other answers are correct. If they are, of course, you must select "all of the above." The same is true for "none."

Remember that the instructions will probably say, "Choose the best answer." Even if you choose "(B) the Andes," and (B) is a correct answer, it gets nuked by "(E) all of the above" if every other answer is also correct.

Chapter 7

The Day of the Exam: 'Psyching Up'

"It is not enough to succeed. Others must fail."
—Gore Vidal (1925—)

"Gore Vidal grades on the curve." —your mother

Well, here you are. No longer are you thinking of the exam as being "next month" or "next week" or even "tomorrow." You're sitting in the very room in the very chair and someone is heading your way with a test paper.

Margaret, lead the way

Right here, right at the beginning of this chapter, let me tell you about my friend Margaret. She's going to help you get there—with a technique I call the Margaret Preview.

Margaret and her husband, Bob, lived in a large capital city in a Third World country. Because of his job, they had to attend a lot of receptions and dinners at other peoples' homes, but the streets of this particular city were not very well marked and the numbering system of the houses was not all that logical.

Bob and Margaret both had a thing about punctuality, so they devised a plan. Early on the day of the party, Margaret, armed with city map and invitation, searched for the house or apartment. And she did not give up until she found it.

Thus, Bob and Margaret would arrive on time without having driven aimlessly around the now-dark streets looking for a house, or a whole neighborhood.

They could have been fashionably late for a party now and then. But you really don't want to be late for a test, especially something like the SAT.

If you're taking a test in a new surrounding, do the Margaret Preview. If it's in a different building or room, take a few minutes and find it. You don't want to discover 90 seconds before the bell that Room 1210A is in the West Tower and not immediately across the hall from Room 1211A in the East Tower where you are standing.

If it's off campus, check out the location a few days early. See how long it takes you (and adjust for weather, time of day and day of the week). Where is the parking? Which door do you go in? Where's the nearest place to get a cup of coffee on the morning of the exam? Is there construction? Which streets are one way? Which exit do you take from the freeway? Are there tolls?

The lifesaving bunch of stuff

Now that you're safely there, on time, what did you bring with you?

I used to make up what I called the Test Kit. Into a backpack went pens or pencils (depending on what I had to have for the test)—two or three of each; the book and workbooks associated with the test; my notes; a calculator, if allowed; a candy bar or other treat that would give me energy; photo ID, if required, and an entry card, if required.

By collecting all this mess in one place, I wouldn't be very likely to forget it. Also, if I did something dreadful like oversleep, I only had to grab the one thing that I had packed the night before and dash, dash, dash out the door.

You have enough to worry you the morning of a big test. Don't spend frantic minutes looking for something that you could have placed inside a backpack or briefcase or large purse the night before. Be kind to yourself.

Double your pleasure—sit alone

Unless you are already in an assigned seat, try to sit near the front so you will get the exam first and have some precious few seconds at the end while the other papers are being passed to the front. It also places you near the teacher or proctor for easier access for questions.

Avoid sitting near someone who has a lot of noisy jewelry, who is cracking or popping gum or who is too friendly with the others in the immediate area. Be a hermit, in other words. Choose a quiet area.

Just a couple more tips: Wear loose, comfortable clothes, the kind that you love, the favorite shirt or sweater or slacks. If you're left-handed, look for a left-handed desk. Check out the room for sunlight (too much or too little), lighting and heat and cold.

The Hoosier measuring system

Remember in the movie "Hoosiers" when the team that Gene Hackman was coaching made it to the state finals? The boys walked into the fieldhouse and were overwhelmed by its size; it sure wasn't like the little gymnasiums they were used to playing in. Gene was smart.

He had them measure the basketball court. Whaddya know? It was exactly the same size as the one back in little Hickory. Point made. Point taken. They won, of course. (Oh, sorry, I thought you'd seen the movie.)

Pull a Gene Hackman. Take a "measure" of the exam in front of you before you begin.

Go all the way

Begin at the beginning. Then move through to the end. No, I'm not talking about taking the exam, I'm talking about looking through the booklet or taking a glance at all the questions. If you have permission to go all the way through it, do that before you ever start. Just give yourself an overview of what lies ahead. That way you can spot the easier sections (and do them first) and get an idea of the point values assigned to each area.

Quick! The Federalist Papers are fading!

First of all, answer those areas where you know the information right now, but you're convinced it is leaking out of your head as you sit there. Go ahead. Get it down.

Then, you usually want to do the easy questions since you can move through them quickly and they will give you a feeling of confidence.

Ask questions immediately if you don't understand something. The proctor may not be able to say anything (or may not know anything to say), but it's worth a try.

If you get part of a question answered and you need to return to finish it but you can't figure it out, work out a little code for yourself. Put a symbol in the margin beside the problem that translates as "I'm partly done here—come back to this one after I've done all the ones I can do."

Guess and guess again?

If you do guess at any of the objective questions and you are getting your test paper returned to you, place a little dot or other symbol beside them. That way you will know how successful your guessing was. For example, suppose you guessed at 30 questions and you got 22 of them right. It says you are making educated guesses for the most part and that you earned enough points to make it worthwhile, even though you got penalized for missing eight others. However, if you only got six right, review my comments on educated guessing. Something's not working right.

When you think you have finished with a whole section, double-check to see if that's true. Look on the answer sheet or in the blue book to make sure all the questions have been answered.

It's time to figure this one out

Pace yourself. If you have 40 multiple-choice questions and you have 20 minutes allotted for that section, you don't have to be MIT material to figure that you should spend a maximum of 30 seconds on each answer. Check your progress two or three times during the 20 minutes.

Which reminds me: Don't depend on a wall clock to tell you the time. Bring your watch. Some students like to remove it and place it on the desk so they can see it without having to look down at their wrist, especially if the writing hand and the watch hand are different.

You say oral and I say aural

Listen up.

When the teacher (or tape recorder) gives you a question, jot down the key words so that you can refer to them when you think up your answer.

Do the same thing if you are being given a dictation where you are expected to listen, then write down what you heard. Key words—the nouns and verbs—will help you "capture" the rest of the sentence.

If you don't understand the question (whether it's in a foreign language you're studying or in English), ask to have it repeated. Ask again if you still don't understand. Listen intently to everything.

For computer-scored tests

If you are required to color in a little rectangle to show which answer is correct so that a machine can score the results, mark the answer sheet very carefully. Stray pencil marks can be picked up by the computer, causing the wrong answer to be recorded. If you carefully filled in one box, only to change your mind later, completely, *completely* erase the first answer. If the computer picks up both markings, guess what happens? You don't get a point, even if one of the boxes is correct.

No post-break dancing, please

Take the breaks that are offered. You'll benefit in the long run by going to the bathroom, getting a drink of water, eating a candy bar, or all of the above, rather than sitting there working through another algebraic equation, if you're allowed to go on working.

Just as you needed the good sleep you got during the week, you'll need to be energized by the breaks. Besides, suppose you didn't move, and then, 20 minutes after the break, you've got to go the bathroom. Desperately. What if the proctor won't let you? Do you kill him and take the SAT while in prison at West Bubba, Arkansas? Or do you act smart and take the break when everyone else does?

They'll never kick sand in your face again

You can perform some unobtrusive exercises at your desk that will make you feel refreshed. Try them right now. First, tense up your feet—squeeze them hard, then relax them, then squeeze them. Do the same with the muscles in your calves, shoulders, hips and abdomen. It's a pretty simple exercise but I find it energizes me when I am unable to get up and move around the room. Even moving the facial muscles helps. Do them looking down at your paper, or otherwise your teacher will think you are making faces at her or that you are having a coronary.

If there is time, review. Go back and check over answers to essay questions that may not be as complete as you'd like them to be, or look again at the unanswered questions in any other section.

If you have even more time, look at the "guess" questions you've marked. Does anything suddenly make sense, making you change your mind? Remember what I said about going with your first choice, but if you suddenly remember that the Catskills are in New York and not in North Dakota, change the answer!

For my next trick

If you've just finished a big, big test, get out of town. Go to a movie or a party or something that will allow you to forget, for a few hours, that you have been keeping your nose to the grindstone for the past several days.

Go. Relax. Then go on to Chapter 8.

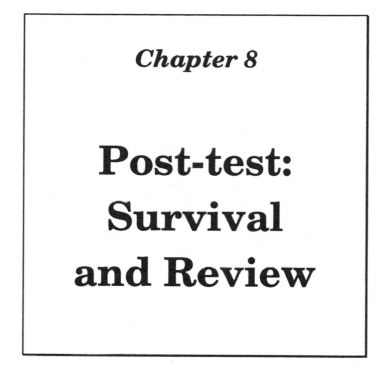

Chapter 8

Post-test: Survival and Review

"*Winning isn't everything, but wanting to win is.*"
—Vince Lombardi (1913-1970)

"*Winning is everything.*" —your mother

No, it's not, Mom. But you and I know what she's talking about, don't we? It's nice to win, whether it's a noontime intramural basketball game or getting an "A" on an exam.

And, don't you agree, it feels even better to "win" when the exam has been tough, when it's been challenging and difficult, than when it was one of Mr. Bibble's easy unit tests.

And Vince got it right. Wanting to win is important. Otherwise, why did you study so hard and give up so much for so long?

Now that you've done the studying and taken the test, you want to know the results. Not all of us are real eager at this point to find out how we did, especially if we're pretty sure we didn't set any records on high scores.

Let's assume you did well. Congratulations! But, no matter how many points you earned, reviewing the test is a vitally important exercise in preparing yourself for the next test—and for taking a hard look at the entire way you study.

If you take a standardized test and you are offered the chance to get a copy of the exam—and your own answers— do so. It may cost you a few bucks, but I definitely think it's worth it.

It's unlikely you'll find they made any mistakes in the scoring of the exam, but it will be good exercise for you to review what you got right and what you didn't while the test is reasonably fresh in your mind.

The emphasis in this chapter, however, is on the tests you take from teachers. Most will review the overall results of the test with the class on the day they are returned. First of all, you want to make sure the answers that you missed are truly incorrect. Teachers make mistakes. I know that's going to come as a shock.

Don't make a nuisance of yourself by challenging everything in class, waving your hand and saying, in a pleading voice, "But, but, Mr. Squeezicks! I meant to say George Washington Carver instead of George Washington"!

Concentrate on the answers that are clearly marked wrong. Even a semi-alert student evaluating his or her own exam can grab a couple of extra points and those points can move you up another letter grade.

If the question really was ambiguous and your answer could arguably be as correct as the one the teacher chose, go ahead and make a pitch. This will be especially effective if a few others in the class chose the same answer. (There is strength in numbers.)

Your chances will be a lot better if you keep the discussion on a diplomatic level, of course, rather than getting snotty or snide. Teachers can get so defensive sometimes!

Now, let's suppose you did get the answer wrong, fair and square. Most likely, you got it wrong for one of these reasons:

You made a careless mistake

1. You wrote down the wrong letter or number. You knew the answer was (A), but, in your haste, you wrote down (B).

2. Similarly, you filled in the wrong box in the answer sheet. You see the mistake now. You vow not to do it again. (Good. That's the first step on the road to recovery.)

3. You left out a whole section of the test because you didn't turn the page, or you "thought" you had done it or...

4. You wrote in such a scribbled fashion or crammed the words together so much that the teacher pulled an "I can't read it so it's wrong" deal on you and gave you no credit. (I'm on his side. Get your act—and your penmanship—together.)

5. You misread the directions. You missed the slightly important word "not," so you provided the exact opposite of what you should have.

6. You guessed wildly without even reading the options and ignored the fact that points would be

deducted for wrong answers, so you got fewer points than if you had left the answer sheet blank for those questions.

You didn't know the material

1. You didn't read all the assignments, or get a complete set of class notes, or find out answers to questions you had about some of the information.
2. You attended class, took notes and read the assignments, but you didn't understand what the topic was all about.
3. You needed to know a lot of facts—dates, names, events, causes and effects—and you didn't.

Your personal life loomed too large

1. You brought into the test your worries that the person you're dating is going to dump you or that your parents are fighting again or...whatever.
2. You had a horrible cold, a terrible headache or you got too little or too much sleep.

Next time I'll know better

Don't beat up on yourself too much. Do take time to evaluate how you did—the bad and the good. Go for the positive. Maybe you always hated essay questions and this time you did well. It's as important to evaluate why you *were* successful as why you *weren't*.

In that case, maybe you learned from your study group. Maybe your teacher gave you some good advice. Maybe you read that section of this book first and it helped you (I like that choice). Maybe you're picking up reading and comprehension skills from a combination of factors. Do think back over what you may have done differently this time. Give yourself a lot of the credit. After all, you took the test all by yourself. Pat-on-the-back time!

The worrisome part is the "careless mistake" area, yet it's probably the easiest to correct, too. Take a vow that you won't do such silly things again. It's especially annoying when you had the right answer and you simply circled the wrong one. Next time? Pay a little closer attention to what you're doing and pace yourself so you can double-check your work.

There's no substitute for knowledge

If you go into the test knowing only half the material, don't expect to get above the 50-percent mark. Doing well on a test, as I've been telling you all along, is a combination of knowing how to take the test and knowing the stuff that goes into the answers.

If you can't seem to get prepared, maybe you'd better go back and reread those earlier chapters. Get to class, get your work organized, manage your time, read the book, do your homework, the whole *shtick*.

Now's the time to see where the teacher got the questions that made up the test. What percentage of the test came from the lectures? From the book? From the handouts?

It is unlikely that you're going to get an "A" in every class you take, but you can get the best grade possible. Even in classes that, for whatever reason, are way, way over your head, you can at least pass. And, in most cases, you're going to do a lot better than that.

Ask questions. Ask questions during class. Ask questions when you meet with your teacher. Join a study group and ask questions. Ask questions when the test results are being discussed.

Pity parties are "out" this year

What nerve you have! A personal life, you say? But isn't Chemistry 104 or American Government more important?

Of course not. But turn the personal motor off now and then and spend time with your friends down at the Continental Congress.

Yes, we all have colds and sore feet and heartbreaks. That is life, after all. But we can compartmentalize the parts of our life now and then without going overboard with it. Remember the Imelda Marcos Theory.

Guess how you did

Don't forget to see how many of your "guesses" you got right. Naturally, the better you know the material, the fewer guesses you need to make, but on some big tests you may have a lot of them.

And the door prize goes to...

After you've sacrificed to get a good grade on the exam, treat yourself. A little fun-and-games reward system is in order. You study really hard for four hours, have a candy bar. You get a B on the quiz over the French Revolution, go to a fun movie.

When you have something to look forward to, even though you realize it's a game (hey, life is a game, so play along!), it makes it "fun" to push yourself in order to kick back and relax.

Let's try that one again, shall we?

If you really messed up on the test, sit down with your teacher and discuss the reasons (having first done your self-evaluation, based on the areas mentioned in this chapter).

Ask if you can take another test—you may not be able to get any credit for it, but you'll impress him and he will look more kindly upon you when it comes time to enter your final grade on the official form.

Retaking "bad" tests is a good idea for another reason. Unless you just completely messed up in getting the right answers matched to the right questions, you probably did so poorly because you didn't know the material well enough the first time.

Now you are giving yourself a second chance to learn material that will no doubt appear on more tests in future, and—now this may come as a real shock—you might actually need to know this information for some reason in your future life.

And, a satisfactory completion of the retake will give you a boost of self-confidence that got stomped on when you got a bad grade the first time. Hey, you're saying to the Test Demons, I can do this!

Come with me now to the inner sanctum

I've been talking to you about what you can and should do. Now, let's take a peek in the next chapter at this whole test business from the teacher's point of view. C'mon, he won't bite.

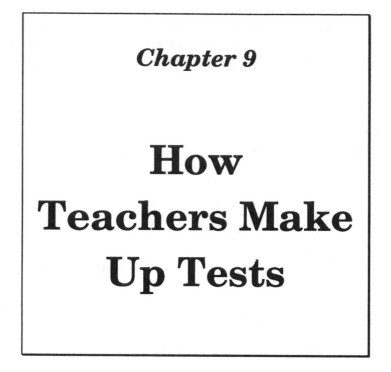

Chapter 9

How Teachers Make Up Tests

"Examinations are formidable even to the best pre-pared, for the greatest fool may ask more than the wisest man can answer." —Charles Caleb Colton (1780?-1832)

Apparently, Mr. Colton had just flunked his mid-term.

You've got one advantage over Colton: You're going to read this chapter and learn how the "greatest fools" make up those tests.

I have to admit that some teachers, I am sorry to report, look upon tests as ways to beat down challenges to their authority ("I'll show them who knows this stuff!") or as punishment ("That'll teach them not to love English lit!"), but fortunately the key word here is "some."

Instead, let's look at how a typical teacher makes up a test.

I'm just an average kind of guy

If students (who have studied and made a valid attempt to do well on the test) earn a test grade that ranges from "excellent" to "good" to "average" (i.e., A to B to C), then this tells them where they stand and it tells the teacher where he stands, too.

If the test results show everyone getting an A or everyone getting Ds and Fs (after honest attempts to do well), the teacher has messed up.

On tests, the majority of students will get Bs and Cs, with a small number getting As and Ds. There should be an even smaller number of Fs, "rewards" for those who truly don't have a clue or who don't care.

The test is, after all, a test of the teacher, too. The teacher has an obligation to give you information, help you understand that information, make assignments that have some validity, and take you progressively through a series of learning exercises.

The test should reflect your understanding of this body of knowledge. The burden is on you to do the work and learn the material; there is an additional burden on the teacher to make sure everyone (except those who don't care) is actually learning.

The wise teacher provides several opportunities during the semester to "test" how well you are learning. Quizzes (scheduled and surprise ones), papers, reports, projects, tests on units, chapters or whole books, oral reports, etc. All of this should add up to your evaluation—your grade.

"Ace" Any Test

Some teachers love one type of question. Some are True-False Freaks; others push the Multiple-Choice/Short Answer Combo. If old tests, old students, the teacher's own comments on the test coming up and your own experience tell you this is true, you might as well study for that kind of test. You still have to know the material, of course. It's just that you may need to remind yourself that you're going to have to deal with it in a particular fashion.

The best teachers use a combination of test questions to find out what you know. Frankly, some of them hate grading essay questions so they rarely use them.

Why do teachers choose essay questions?

1. They are easier and less time-consuming to prepare.
2. They may be preferred when a group is small and the test will not be reused.
3. They are used to explore student's attitudes rather than measure his or her achievements.
4. They are used to encourage and reward the development of student skill in writing.
5. They are suitable when it's important for the students to explain or describe.
6. They are more suitable to some material. You're likely to have more essay questions in English and history than you are in the sciences, and vice versa.

Teachers use objective questions because:

1. They are preferred when the group is large and the test may be reused.
2. They are more efficient when highly reliable test scores must be obtained quickly.

3. They are more suitable for covering a larger amount of content in the same amount of time.
4. They are easier for the teacher to give an impartial grade. Whether it's the good student or the bad, the good essay writer or the lousy one, everyone has to write down (C) to get number 22 correct.
5. They are easier for some teachers to create.
6. They may be used when students need to demonstrate or show.

A thousand points of right

At the time that the teacher decides what kinds of questions he will ask and determines what each question will cover, he must also assign a point value to each question.

He is going to assign higher point values to questions that are concerned with material that has been emphasized by his lectures and class discussions and by the reading. He will also assign more points to areas of the test that will require more time and attention.

Think about it: You've never taken a test where each true-false question was worth 20 points and the long essay was worth five. He will clearly show the points possible for each section and/or question so you can decide how to spend your time.

Teachers have check lists, too

The teacher has selected the material to be covered. He's told you, at least in general terms, what the test will be over. He has decided on the format of the test, assigned points and written the questions, then done his own double-checking to make sure he has included everything he wanted to include.

He has also made sure that the questions this semester are different from the ones on previous tests as he suspects that some of you little devils will be looking at them, hoping against hope that he will provide the same questions again.

He has set up the test in a readable format so there is no confusion, and has made sure it is free of typos. He has checked his questions and answers to make sure they are not ambiguous.

Should we give him a passing grade?

The "test" for him comes when he sits down to grade what you've done. If half the students completely messed up one of the questions—but messed it up in the same way—he has to admit that the directions were not clearly written. He may even decide to throw out the question.

He has determined that the number and complexity of the questions are suitable for the time allotted for the test. If he consistently finds that even his best students only completed half the test, he had too much on the test. And, hopefully, will shorten future ones.

A key word that the teacher has to remind himself to use in making up and in grading a test is "reasonable." What is a *reasonable* number of questions students can be expected to answer in 45 minutes? What should a teacher *reasonably* expect students to know from these chapters?

You can learn to fake sincerity

No, you can't. I just said that to keep your attention. In this chapter on teachers, let me leave you with this thought about your relationship with those who instruct you:

Teachers do like students (and give them better grades) if they show a genuine interest in the subject matter and in the class. You don't have to be a total Teacher's Pet or Nerd of the Month. But you should feel free to show that you like what you're learning.

And if you've decided that chemistry is far down on your dislike list along with public speaking and serious leg cramps, don't vent your anger, hatred and snide remarks to your teacher. Look. He loves this stuff. He even goes to conventions where there are other chemistry teachers. He spends his weekends reading books like *50 Ways to Make Milkshakes with Hydrochloric Acid*. Just endure. Do the best you can. Smile. And—best of all—go to him with honest questions about material that you can't or don't understand. He's there to help you.

Fill in the blank so you won't go blank

I'll leave you with one more thing—the item I referred to back in Chapter 4. On the next page is the form that I've designed to help you sort out what you've got to do when, where and how.

Stop! Don't fill this out. Photocopy it, then fill in the blanks.

There. I've said it. I'm done. And you're just getting started.

Remember this: Don't ever say again, "She gave me a C!" No, she didn't. Your teachers don't give you grades. You give yourself grades. The C (or A or D) you earned on the last test was given to yourself by yourself.

So, what are you going to give yourself this next time?

PRE-TEST ORGANIZER

CLASS:_____ TEACHER: _____

TEST DATE:_____TIME: From _____to _____

PLACE:_____

SPECIAL INSTRUCTIONS to myself (e.g., take calculator, dictionary, etc.):_____

MATERIALS I NEED to study for this test (check all needed):

    ❑ Book   ❑ Tapes/Videos
    ❑ Workbook   ❑ Old Tests
    ❑ Class Notes   ❑ Other
    ❑ Handouts   ❑ _____

THE FORMAT of the test will be (write the number of T/F, essays, mult.-choice, etc., and total points for each section):

_____

_____

_____

_____

_____

STUDY GROUP MEETINGS (times, places):

1._____

2._____

3._____

MATERIAL TO BE COVERED:
Indicate topics, sources and amount of review (light or heavy) required. Check box when review is completed.

Topic	Sources	Review
_____	_____	❑ _____
_____	_____	❑ _____
_____	_____	❑ _____
_____	_____	❑ _____
_____	_____	❑ _____
_____	_____	❑ _____
_____	_____	❑ _____
_____	_____	❑ _____
_____	_____	❑ _____

AFTER THE TEST:
Grade I expected _____ Grade I received _____

What did I do that helped me? _____

_____

_____

_____

What else should I have done?

_____

_____

_____

_____

Index

"Ace"
Any
Test

"All of the above," multiple-
    choice, 69
Analogies, objective tests,
    62-63
Anxiety,
    pre-test, 7-13
    reducing, 11-13
Assignments, 34-36
    due, 24
    how to read, 34-36

Big Picture, value of Term
    Planning Calendar, 21

Class, 28-36
    going to, 29
    how to prepare, 30
    importance of, 29
    taking notes, 31
Colton, Charles Caleb, 84
Competition, 9-10
Comprehension questions,
    objective tests, 64-66
Computer-scored tests, 75

Daily schedule,
    importance of, 27

Daily Schedule form, 19
 categories, 24-25
 how to use, 24
 sample, 25

Dante, 28
de Secondat, Charles, 37
Deadlines, Term Planning
 Calendar, 21

Essay tests, 49-56
 conclusion, 53
 introduction, 53
 leaving space, 55
 outline, sample, 51-52
 proofreading, 55-56
 quality before
  quantity, 52
 review before
  beginning, 50
 sample answer, 53-55
 why teachers give, 86

Facsimile test, 41
Fear,
 of fear itself, 7
 of success, 9
 value of, 8
Flash cards, test
 preparation, 40

Grade ranges, 85
Guessing,
 how to, 59-60
 objective tests, 58

High priorities, time
 management, 18
Homework, Daily
 Schedule, 26

Improve Your Reading, 34
Inverted Pyramid
 Theory, 24, 38

Johnson, Samuel, 49

Lists, advantages of
 making, 17
Lombardi, Vince, 77
Low priorities, time
 management, 18

Manage Your Time,
 15f, 18
Margaret Preview, 71
Matching questions,
 objective tests, 67
Math questions, objective
 tests, 67-68
Medium priorities, time
 management, 18
Mistakes,
 learning from, 81
 most common, 79-80
Mnemonics,
 definition of, 42
 example, 42-43
Multiple-choice questions,
 tips, 61-62
 "all of the above," 69
 "none of the above," 69

"None of the above,"
    multiple-choice, 69
Notes,
    abbreviating words, 33
    friends', 32
    handwriting, 33
    how to take good, 33
    importance of, 32
    taking own, 32
    too few, 33
    too many, 32

Objective tests, 57-67
    analogies, 62-63
    comprehension
        questions, 64-66
    drawing pictures,
        symbols, 60
    guessing, 58
    math questions, 67-68
    sentence completion, 68
    vocabulary, 68-69
    why teachers give, 86
Outline, essay tests, 50

Parkinson, Cyril, 14
Pictures, symbols, objective
    tests, 60
Point values, 87
Pop quizzes, 30-31
Post-test,
    review, 77-83
    standardized tests, 78
Pre-Test Organizer, 39
    sample, 90-91
Priorities,
    setting, 18

Term Planning
    Calendar, 21
Priority Tasks This
    Week, 24
    form, 19
    how to use, 22
    questions to ask, 22
    sample, 23
Projects Board, 19

Quizzes, surprise, 30-31

Reading,
    assignments, 34-36
    main points in text, 35
    maps, charts, etc. 35
    reviewing, 35-36
Review for class, when to, 36
Roosevelt, Franklin
    Delano, 7

SAT,
    content, 46
    determining
        weaknesses, 45
    Mathematics Level
        IIC, 48
    new components, 47
    preparation
        courses, 45-46
    review, 45
    studying for, 44-46
SAT-I, 47-48
SAT-II, 47ff
Scanning,
    definition of, 39
    test preparation, 39

Schedule, 26
  being realistic, 27
  importance of, 27
  when to check, 26
Sentence completion,
  objective tests, 68
Skimming,
  definition of, 39
  test preparation, 39
Standardized tests, post-
  test, 78
Study groups,
  choosing participants, 40
  how to use, 41
  test preparation, 40

Take Notes, 31, 33
Teachers,
  assigning points to
    questions, 87
  favorite types of
    questions, 86
  grade ranges, 85
  how they make up tests,
    84-89
  making points with, 88
  test preparation, 43-44
  tested by their exams, 85
  why they give essay
    exams, 86
  why they give objective
    tests, 86
Tension, value of, 8
Term Planning
  Calendar, 18, 24
  how to use, 19
  sample, 20

Test anxiety, 7-13
  reducing, 11, 13
Test breaks,
  exercises, 76
  taking advantage of, 75
Test day, 70-76
  choosing a seat, 72
  getting there, 71
  what to bring, 72
Test preparation,
  flash cards, 40
  materials needed, 38
  scanning, 39
  skimming, 39
  study groups, 40
  studying old exams, 42
  teachers, 43-44
Test taking,
  breaks, 75
  computer-scored
    tests, 75
  guessing, 74
  how to, 73-76
  pacing, 74
Tests,
  competition, 9-10
  concentrating on, 10
  essays, 49-56
  failure, 9
  most common
    mistakes, 79-80
  multiple choice, 61-62
  objective, 57-67
  point values, 87
  preparing for, 13
  retaking, 82
  studying for, 38-48

taking extra, 12
test teachers too, 85
Time management, 14-27
big business, 15
To do/errands, Daily
Schedule, 26
To-do lists,
importance of, 26

time management, 16

Vidal, Gore, 70
Vocabulary, objective
tests, 68-69

Woolf, Virginia, 49